T0146648

Cherished
Memories

Poems and Short Stories

By Cindy Young

Inspiring Voices books may be ordered through booksellers or by contacting:

Inspiring Voices
1663 Liberty Drive
Bloomington, IN 47403
www.inspiringvoices.com
1-(866) 697-5313

Because of the dynamic nature of the Internet, any web addresses or links contained in this book may have changed since publication and may no longer be valid. The views expressed in this work are solely those of the author and do not necessarily reflect the views of the publisher, and the publisher hereby disclaims any responsibility for them.

Any people depicted in stock imagery provided by Thinkstock are models, and such images are being used for illustrative purposes only. Certain stock imagery © Thinkstock.

ISBN: 978-1-4624-0776-7 (sc)
ISBN: 978-1-4624-0777-4 (e)

Printed in the United States of America

Inspiring Voices rev. date: 2/4/2014

Introduction

I grew up in a small town in Idaho where things that matter are family, friends, holidays, and our pets. I wrote this book of poetry and short stories showing my passion for the simple life. My book is inspirational and will take you to a time of love and treasured memories of the past.

Cindy Young

I was like a ship lost at sea,
You were the beacon that guided me back to shore

By Cindy Young

Spring

The flowers peek their heads
Out of a light veil of snow,
They look for the sunlight
To help them grow.

The days are getting longer
With a promise of Spring,
If you take time to listen
You'll hear the birds sing.

It's been a long winter
Seems it would never end,
But
Spring is here to greet us
Like a long lost friend.

By Cindy Young

The
Beauty of
Spring

Spring is here once again to rescue us from the cold days of winter. With it comes a renewal. The grass turns green and the days are longer and warmer. The familiar flowers of the season push their way out of the ground, anxious to show off their beauty after a long slumber in the cold grip of winter.

The animals and birds give birth to their babies and bask in the sunlight to keep warm. They too, are glad for the change.

Oh - - - the beauty of Spring! She is a gift to us all saying, "I am here at last to usher in my sister Summer."

By Cindy Young

Easter

Easter is an important day in my family. When I was a child we would all get a new set of clothes and dress up for church. I got a new dress, shoes and a hat. After church we would come home and hunt for eggs. I was the youngest and didn't do so well filling my basket with eggs so reluctantly, my siblings would share theirs with me.

My mother would cook a cherry glazed ham and potato salad. We would eat our meal and spend some time outside if it was nice.

Easter is a time to thank God for making it through a long, hard winter. It's also a time of joy for the change in the weather and the renewal of the land.

By Cindy Young

Summer

I love the long days of Summer
The walks in the park,
Sitting on my porch
Till long after dark.

The cool gentle breeze
At the end of the day,
The scent of the roses
Blooming by the way.

Riding my bicycle
Up and down the lane,
The feel of the raindrops
Getting caught in the rain.

Of all the things mentioned
What I love best,
Is laying on my hammock
Taking a rest.

By Cindy Young

My mother, next to garden and flowers

My Garden

I love to plant my garden
My seeds are in a row,
I give them lots of water
And weed them with a hoe.

Soon the seeds I've planted
Push out of the ground,
They grow bigger every day
What a miracle I have found.

Lots of fresh vegetables
I will harvest until fall,
Knowing I grew my own garden
Is the pleasure of it all.

By Cindy Young

The Rose

She comes in any color
That you would want to see,
Her scent is unforgettable
As it was meant to be.

She stands tall and majestic
As she guards her domain,
Her beauty is regal
Yet she is never vain.

One thing I am sure of
And most everybody knows,
No flower can compare to
Her majesty, *The Rose.*

By Cindy Young

Fourth of July

It's the 4th of July
In our country so grand,
Let's bring out the flag
And strike up the band.

There's a parade and a carnival
Music and food for everyone,
So bring all the family
And have lots of fun.

We will end the fine day
With a fireworks show,
And watch the night sky
Light up with sparkle and glow.

By Cindy Young

Autumn

A hint of Autumn
is in the air,
The days are shorter
but I don't care.

The leaves are turning
crimson and gold,
Demanding our attention
They are vivid and bold.

The Harvest moon
is big and bright,
It lights up the sky
on a cool, calm night.

Though winter is coming
I have no dread,
The memory of Autumn
lingers in my head.

By Cindy Young

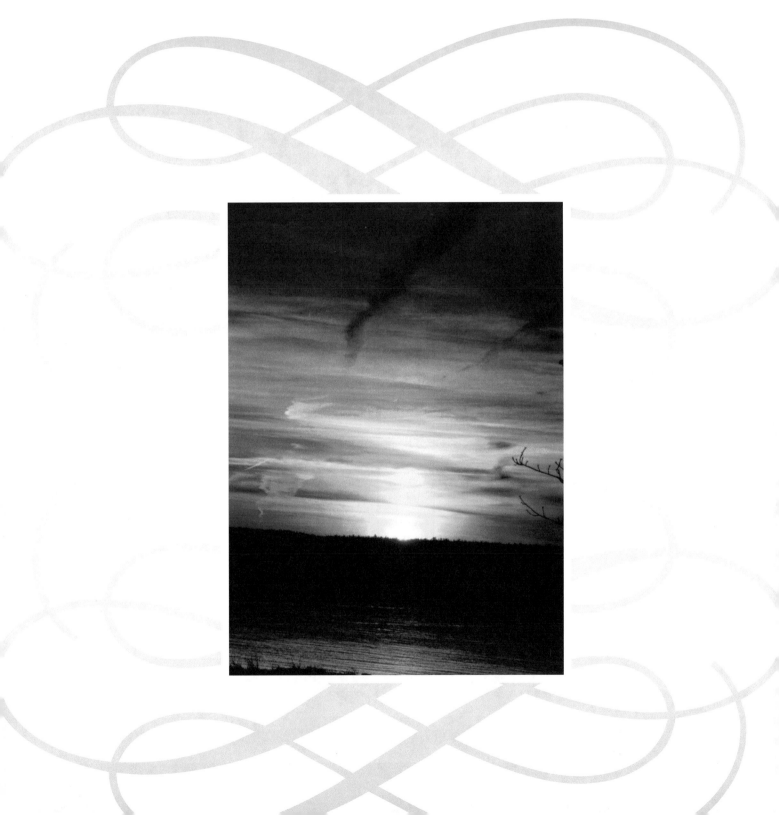

Fall

When the sunset is blazing
Like a fire in the sky,
We look up in wonder
But never ask why.

The leaves change colors
As they hang from the trees,
They fall to the ground
With a cool gentle breeze.

The farmers are busy
With their harvest abound,
Apples, pumpkins, and gourds
Lay all around.

When all this happens
We know fall is here,
For me
This is the most beautiful
Time of the Year.

By Cindy Young

Halloween

Ghosts and goblins
Are coming out tonight,
They're all looking for candy
So there is no reason for fright.

All the kids are anxious
To get out of school,
They are going trick-or-treating
Until their bags are full.

So if you see something spooky
Standing at your door,
Get out your bowl of candy
That's what they're looking for.

By Cindy Young

The House

Let me tell you a story
About a house on the hill,
Empty and foreboding
Projecting ill will.

It was said to be haunted
But I went there on a bet,
I got there at midnight
A night I'll not forget.

As I walked close to the house
The yard was ever so bare,
Soon I could smell the scent
Of jasmine in the air.

As I crept even closer
I could hear music from inside,
It was music from the past
Though afraid, I would abide.

I saw a light in a window
I drew closer and peeked in,
I heard a voice out of the darkness
Ask, "Where have you been?"

The figure of a lady
Was dancing by candle light,
Moving like a feather
All dressed in white.

As I turned and ran away
My heart pounding from fright,
I heard a faint whisper say,
"Come dance with me some night."

By Cindy Young

Thanksgiving

As we sit at our dining room table
The scent of turkey is in the air,
We bow our heads in reverence
To say our Thanksgiving prayer.

We thank God for all our blessings
And our family, Oh so dear,
We take a moment to remember
Those who are not here.

We ask God to guide us
In everything we do,
And always stay beside us
For we depend on you.

By Cindy Young

Winter

Winter is a majestic time of the year.
The trees are like sleeping giants weighted down
with snow and ice. They await the warm rays of the sun to
free them from their heavy load.
As we look out over the land on a moonlit night,
the clouds move slowly across the sky casting shadows
over the glistening snow, sparkling like diamonds.
Winter is a time to relax at home and reflect on the
good times spent with your loved ones. It's a time to
dream and make plans for the future.
Winter is a burden for some, but for me it's a
time to slow down and enjoy the beauty of it all.

By Cindy Young

Your Gift

It's not wrapped in pretty paper
It's not underneath your tree,
It's not something you can touch
Or something you can see.

Your gift is something special
But it did not cost a lot,
Your gift is my love and friendship
For that is all I've got.

By Cindy Young

My Best Gift

Christmas is here once again and now that I am older most of my family have moved away and are no longer here. I spend some of my Holidays alone now, but I refuse to be sad as now my Christmas consists of mostly cards, decorations and cherished memories of Christmas spent with my loved ones.

I have one Christmas memory that I hold close to my heart and would like to share with you. I was six years old in 1952. Times were difficult for our family. With five siblings my father's paycheck did not go far. That Christmas I made it known that I wanted a toy piano, but I knew we were poor and therefore Santa must be poor.

I went to bed Christmas Eve with great anticipation what Santa might bring, maybe a doll, a pretty dress or some toy dishes would be nice. I awoke at dawn and ran to the Christmas tree lit with bright beautiful lights. The presents were wrapped in pretty paper and stacked neatly under the tree. Our stockings were also filled to the brim.

To my great surprise, in the midst of all the gifts was a toy piano. Overwhelmed with excitement, I ran to "my" piano. It was just the right size for me with a small stool to sit on. Immediately I started tapping out tunes. The first song I learned to play was *"Mary had a Little Lamb."* I played my piano most of the day. I was certain I would be able to play in a concert some day for I knew I was a pro. Looking back, I don't think my parents shared my enthusiasm and were relieved when I gave it up and went to bed that evening.

Well needless to say, I was not a pro and never played in a concert. I later lost interest in the piano and moved on to other things. But truly this was the best gift I ever received as a child, and I will never forget the joy it gave to me.

By Cindy Young

My Mother, Phyllis 1930

My Mother

How can I ever thank you
For all that you have done,
Whenever I needed refuge
To you, I would always run.

You never longed for fortune
You never longed for fame,
To take care of your family
Was your only aim.

You are oh so dear to me
There will never be another,
No one can ever take the place
Of you, my sweet Mother.

By Cindy Young

My Son, Delbert 1965

My Son

I don't often tell you
How much you mean to me,
I am glad that I am your mother
And proud as I can be.

You're such a kind and gentle person
With a loving heart,
You're everything you should be
And you were right from the start.

No matter where you go, Son
Or whatever you may do,
Remember…
You are someone special
And I always will love you!

By Cindy Young

My Companion

I have a companion
As cute as she can be,
She's a little hairy
But that doesn't bother me.

She has big brown eyes
Floppy ears and a wet nose,
And she wags her tail
Wherever she goes.

She is very lazy
But I don't mind,
She is my dog Pee Wee
The best friend I can find.

By Cindy Young

My Friend

I have a special friend
Who is always there for me,
She is a very loving person
And sweet as she can be.

When I need someone to listed
She will always lend an ear,
Even if it's something
She doesn't want to hear.

She laughs when I am happy
She comforts me when I am sad,
She always understands
And calms me when I am mad.

I know it's very common
For us all to have a friend,
But I know she will always be there
Right up until the end.

By Cindy Young

My Love

I had a special love once
He was everything to me,
Forever close beside him
Is where I longed to be.

I longed to hold him close
And gaze into his eyes,
He was there to guide me
As was oh so wise.

I always felt protected
When I was by his side,
We would walk together
My heart would fill with pride.

Then one day, he went away
I never did know why,
I had a special love once
Now I sit and cry.

By Cindy Young

Forever In Our Hearts

You've been gone some time now
We still miss you so,
For you are someone special
And were very nice to know.

We miss the sound of your laughter
And your kind and gentle touch,
The way you cared for us
We miss that oh so much.

We miss the way you loved us
And always let it show,
The comfort that you gave us
You will never know.

Even though we still shed a tear
Because you went away,
We know you are in Heaven
And we will see you again someday.

By Cindy Young

Cherished Memories

It is amazing how wonderful a clear mind can be. I am in my sixties and my body is falling apart but my mind is still in tact. I forget names and lose my train of thought when talking but I have a very clear memory of when I was growing up. I often sit in my favorite chair and think back to simpler and happier times when I was young.

I come from a poor family. I am the youngest of six children. My father worked long and hard hours to feed and clothe us. He was a farmhand and was paid very little for his hard work. We moved many times as we followed him wherever my father's job was. Then one day he got a "steady" job at a potato processing plant in Idaho. It was a good paying job so he decided it was now time to buy a house. Needless to say we were all very happy. No more moving. We could finally settle into a home of our own.

The house we chose was not much to look at and needed a lot of work. With just one bedroom and no indoor bathroom, it would have scared most people away at first sight; but my father knew it was a diamond in the rough. He quickly went to work painting indoors and out. He chose sky blue with white trim for the outside. He shingled the roof then started on the yard. He made a white picket fence for the front yard. Later he added on a bedroom for my two brothers. Three of my older siblings had already left by this time. He also built a bathroom. That was a memorable event, no more going to the outhouse. We were all thrilled!

My father was a very ambitious man. He planted a big garden in the backyard and took care of it by himself. He also planted several rows of zinnias beside the picket fence in the front yard. The flowers were in full bloom by July and people often stopped to admire the flowers and the garden.

One of my favorite things about the backyard was an old shed that my father gave to me for a playhouse. He cut a square hole in the front and covered it with plastic to let in the light. He painted it blue to match the house. I was given an old couch and table. I put up some old curtains and I acquired an old lamp, some pictures and many other items to make my playhouse like a real home. I spent many happy hours there with my neighborhood friends until I became a teenager.

If I could go back in time and relive one day from the past it would be one of the summer Saturday afternoons when my family gathered beneath a big elm tree in front of our house. My two teenage brothers entertained us playing their guitars and singing Johnny Cash songs. My mother fried chicken and made corn on the cob, red potatoes and peas, and salad; all vegetables from the garden. *My married siblings, their kids and some cousins stopped by for the afternoon. Whoever stopped by never left hungry. We visited, laughed, and sang until evening, united as family at our blue house on Conant Avenue.*

These are some cherished memories I can fall back on when I am having a rough day. For now, they are very vivid in my mind.

By Cindy Young

My Father, Claude 1930

Printed in the United States
By Bookmasters